Praise for *Your Dog's*

This book is filled to the brim with new and wonderfully practical information and advice. In her usual direct and humorous style, Dr. Kay has once again established herself to be a stellar advocate for successful communication between pet owners and their vets.
—Dr. Marty Becker, Featured Columnist Vetstreet.com and Veterinary Contributor for Good Morning America and the Dr. Oz Show

Brilliant! Everyone who has a dog should have a copy of this concise and useful book. Dogs (and vets) everywhere will thank Dr. Nancy for writing it.
—Patricia B. McConnell, PhD, CAAB, Author, *The Other End of the Leash* and *For the Love of a Dog*.

So many of the complaints I hear from family members and friends about their veterinarians could be prevented if only these dog-loving consumers read *Your Dog's Best Health*. Put into practice, Dr. Kay's sensible and informed advice about achieving "a dozen reasonable things to expect from your vet" can help any guardian get the most value for their veterinary health care dollar. Importantly, Dr. Kay's advice will also protect and preserve the lines of communication and trust between the veterinarian and his client, thus maximizing the benefits to the all-important patient.
—Nancy Kerns, Editor, The Whole Dog Journal

The author of *Speaking for Spot* has done it again! Dr. Nancy Kay pulls no punches as she educates us about what we are entitled to as consumers of veterinary medicine. This book belongs on the shelves of dog lovers everywhere. Dr. Kay continues to be our best friend when it comes to advocating for our dogs' health. We have a lot to thank her for!
—Claudia Kawczynska, Editor, The BARK Magazine

There is no one in the veterinary world today advocating more powerfully for clear communication between pet owner and veterinarian than Dr. Nancy Kay. In *Your Dog's Best Health: A Dozen Reasonable Things to Expect From Your Vet*, she cuts through misconceptions and false assumptions to lay out a simple blueprint to guide vet and owner to an effective working relationship and the best possible outcome for every dog.
—Christie Keith, "Your Whole Pet" Columnist, San Francisco Chronicle/ SFGate.com

Today, regardless of whether you have a family pet, performance athlete, or show dog, obtaining individualized, quality veterinary care for your dog requires a new kind of interactive working partnership with your veterinarian. In clear, concise, and award-winning style, *Your Dog's Best Health* clarifies both what you should expect from your veterinarian and what she should expect from you as together you manage your dog's care at the various stages of his life. This is essential reading for anyone who loves a dog.

—Nancy P. Melone, Ph.D., Editor-in-Chief, The Alpenhorn

Few veterinarians have the credentials, skill and knowledge of Dr. Nancy Kay, and fewer still have the gift for sharing what they know to help pet lovers get the best care for their animals. A paragraph by Dr. Kay is worth a celebration. Another book? A bargain at any price, full of passion, compassion and easy-to-understand knowledge you can use to work with your own veterinarian.

—Gina Spadafori, Syndicated Pet-Care Columnist and Author, *Dogs For Dummies*

Dr. Kay's abiding love of people and pets as well as her vibrant enthusiasm for her profession come shining through in this wonderful new book. Encouraging open communication and highlighting reasonable expectations on both sides of the exam table, Dr. Kay plots a takeoff-to-landing course for today's empowered and informed pet-loving public.

—Dr. Tony Johnson, Veterinary Emergency and Critical Care Specialist

As a dog trainer, I am constantly coaching my clients on how to communicate with their veterinarians and become more involved in their pet's medical care. Dr. Kay has made my life so much easier- now all I have to do is tell them to get a copy of *Your Dog's Best Health*. What a help this book will be for dog owners everywhere.

—Turid Rugaas, Professional Dog Trainer and Author, *On Talking Terms with Dogs: Calming Signals*

In *Speaking for Spot*, and now in *Your Dog's Best Health* Dr. Nancy Kay shares expert tips on how pet caregivers can optimize communication with their veterinarian. What better advice than from one who knows – her suggestions are easy to understand and practical. Dr. Kay empowers you to advocate for your pet's health as well as your own peace of mind.

—Jane R. Shaw, DVM, PhD, Director of the Argus Institute, Colorado State University

Dr. Kay is the ultimate pet advocate. This book is a must-read for any dog lover interested in excellent pet care. Her nuggets of wisdom will empower you every time you visit a veterinary clinic so you can take a more active role in your dog's care.

—Dr. Phil Zeltzman, Veterinary Surgeon and Author, *Walk a Hound, Lose a Pound*

We hear a lot about 'the human animal bond' and certainly Nancy Kay is a champion of that relationship - but where her special skills shine is in her books, which speak to the "guardian-vet bond." She has blazed a trail to enhance communication between people and their pets' veterinarians. Dr. Kay's contribution is enormous and her new book is a must-have on the shelf of every vet and the people whose pets are served by them.

—Tracie Hotchner, Author, *The Dog Bible* **and** *The Cat Bible and* **Host of Radio Shows "DOG TALK®" and "CAT CHAT®"**

I wish this book was out when I was dealing with the different health issues that my two 4-legged "sons" have been through. This is a must have for everyone who values their dog as a family member.

—Tamar Geller, Author, *The Loved Dog* **and** *30 Days To A Well-Mannered Dog*

It is so important for pet parents to know that they can be with their beloved animal companions at the very end of their pet's life. Death is the ultimate scary experience - the great unknown. It is so important for Dr. Kay to empower pet owners with information so that they may face the end of their pets' life from a fact-based, versus a fear-based perspective. Thank you, Dr. Kay!

—Dr. Robin Downing, Veterinary Pain Management and Rehabilitation Specialist

Praise for *Speaking for Spot*

There's just so much good about this book, and it is such an important resource for those of us who consider our dogs to be family. I love Nancy's thoughtful and compassionate voice, and couldn't agree more with her encouragement to all of us to be active advocates for our pets' veterinary care.

—Patricia McConnell, PhD, Author, *The Other End of the Leash* and *For the Love of a Dog*

Speaking for Spot is an engaging, compelling and truly indispensable book. Dr. Nancy Kay enables her readers to become well-informed advocates for their pets' health care decisions. She has provided the perfect guide that will make a tremendous difference for dogs and for the people who love them.

—Claudia Kawczynska, Editor-in-Chief, BARK Magazine

Dr. Nancy Kay explains the basics of responsible healthcare and what dog owners should know. But she also illustrates how owners must manage their vet/client relationship, and be assertive advocates for their dogs, for the best possible results. In her chapter on "Finding Dr. Wonderful," the list of "deal breakers" (including "The vet vaccinates dogs for everything, every year.") is worth the price of the book.

—Nancy Kerns, Editor, Whole Dog Journal

From vaccinations and pet insurance to second opinions and end of life decisions, dog lovers often feel overwhelmed trying to make the best choice for their pup, pocket book, and peace-of-mind. Thanks to *Speaking for Spot*, we finally have a book that makes sense of it all! With experience, warmth, wit, and candor, Dr. Nancy Kay provides an authentic, user-friendly guide for making all types of health care choices for your dog.

—Dr. Marty Becker, Resident Veterinarian on Good Morning America and the Dr. Oz Show

This is the book I wish I had when dogs first entered my life. It's the other best friend you need when making routine veterinary decisions for your dog or potentially heart-breaking ones.

—-Amy Tan, Author, New York Times bestsellers *The Joy Luck Club* and *The Kitchen God's Wife*

This book should be in the library of every person who loves her dog. With clarity, charm, and wit, Dr. Kay provides step-by-step guidelines that teach you how to be a responsible and informed advocate throughout your dog's life. It could save you thousands of dollars and give you the tools to prevent the heartache that comes with making uninformed or rushed decisions about your dog's health care.

—Linda Tellington-Jones, Animal Behaviorist and Author, *Getting in* *Touch with Your Dog, Getting in Touch with Your Puppy,* **and** *Unleash Your* *Dog's Potential*

Get this book. I would give this book six stars if I could. It is a valuable tool for pet lovers and veterinarians alike. Dr. Kay offers a wealth of information that is easy to read, memorable and even humorous at times. The appendices of symptoms and diseases are packed with information and could really be their own book. They are cross-referenced to the main book for additional questions to ask your veterinarian, and when applicable, information on veterinary anesthesia and surgery.

-Dr. Janet Tobiassen Crosby, Author, About.com Guide to Veterinary Medicine

If a dog owner could have only 1 book for health information, this is it. This is not a do-it-yourself medical text; rather, it explains how to find the right veterinarian and become a partner in the decision-making process. A unique problem-based approach to 43 common clinical signs helps owners know what to look for and what information a veterinarian needs. The next chapter provides short explanations on > 200 diseases, with questions an owner might ask. Both of these chapters are up to date and clearly written. This is an excellent book at a reasonable price. I highly recommend it.

—Dr. Susan Cotter, Specialist in Internal Medicine and Oncology, Faculty, Tufts College of Veterinary Medicine.

It is easy to write overly sentimental 'fluff' about dogs. It is much harder to write consistent, strong, useful information that is actually helpful. Dr. Kay's insightful *Speaking for Spot* is a comprehensive, long-needed work. I know of no other book of its kind for the American public that tackles the topic in such detail. *Speaking for Spot* is of tremendous practical value to dog lovers and should be mandatory reading for veterinarians.

- Dr. Kevin Fitzgerald, Veterinarian

YOUR DOG'S BEST HEALTH

A Dozen Reasonable Things
to Expect From Your Vet

DR. NANCY KAY

Specialist, American College
of Veterinary Internal Medicine

Author, *Speaking for Spot: Be the Advocate
Your Dog Needs to Live a Happy, Healthy, Longer Life*

www.SpeakingForSpot.com

Foreword by Michael Cavanaugh, DVM
Executive Director
American Animal Hospital Association

Photographs by Susannah Kay
SusannahKay.com

First published in 2011

CreateSpace

Copyright © 2011 Nancy Kay

Printed in United States of America

Disclaimer of Liability

This book is not to be used in place of veterinary care and expertise. The author and publisher shall have neither liability nor responsibility to any person or entity with respect to any loss or damage caused or alleged to be caused directly or indirectly by the information contained in this book. While the book is as accurate as the author can make it, there may be errors, omissions, and inaccuracies.

At the time of publication, the Web addresses featured in this book refer to existing Web sites on the Internet. The author is not responsible for the content on referred-to sites, including outdated, inaccurate, or incomplete information.

Library of Congress Cataloging-in-Publication Data is available.

ISBN 13: 978-1466381957

Book design by Dr. Nancy Kay

Jacket design by CreateSpace

Typefaces: Novarese, Hypatia Sans, Vag Rounded

10 9 8 7 6 5 4 3 2 1

For my patient and wonderful husband Alan who wonders if I will ever run out of words.

Contents

Reasonable Expectations

Acknowledgements

Kate Dederichs and I first met when I began caring for her wonderful dogs. Kate is the kind of client who makes any veterinarian's work a pleasure. She is an active, informed medical advocate for her beloved animals and she treats every member of the hospital staff with genuine gratitude and respect. When Kate learned that I was in the process of writing my first book, *Speaking for Spot*, her enthusiastic response prompted me to ask her to read an early draft in order to provide a "client's perspective." The rest is history. Kate's passion for empowering people to become better medical advocates for their four-legged family members rivals my own. Kate has assisted my writing career in so many ways (simply listing them would require an entire chapter), and in the process, she has become one of my dearest friends. Needless to say, she has done a tremendous amount of work behind the scenes of *Your Dog's Best Health*. Kate is a phenomenally generous and talented woman and I am so grateful for her kindness, friendship, and support.

Lucky me- my daughter Susannah happens to be a gifted

photographer (no, I'm not biased) who loves animals just as much as her two veterinarian parents do. It's a good thing I taught her to share when she was a youngster because she enthusiastically offered forth her delightful dog photos for this book. I am deeply appreciative and one very proud mama.

Special thanks and love to my husband Alan who has learned to live with this writing habit of mine. Not only does he tolerate the incessant clicking of my computer keyboard, he readily picks up the slack in terms of domestic duties when I am in "writing mode." And he's simply the best at providing just the right synonym for any word or phrase I throw his way!

Lastly, thanks to the countless people I've known who have allowed me the privilege of caring for their pets. My clients are my inspiration and I learn something new from them each and every day.

Foreword

If you are reading this, I'll bet you share your life with a pet. What is it about our animals that make us so willing to take care of them, in sickness and in health? The answer is simple. They give us so much in return.

If your pet becomes sick, there are a number of factors that go into making him or her well again. The severity of the disease process, your pet's age and overall health, your veterinarian's expertise, and your ability to care for your pet at home all play a role in whether or not your pet will recover. What you may not realize is that the way you and your veterinarian communicate with each other is a key ingredient in creating a positive outcome, both in terms of your pet's health as well as your own peace of mind. You are an important member of your pet's health care team.

Dr. Nancy Kay is passionate about enhancing communication between veterinarians and the pet owners they serve. In *Speaking for Spot* she taught us why we need to be medical advocates for our pets and how to fulfill this important role. In *Your Dog's Best Health* she continues our education by clearly spelling out what is reasonable for pet owners to expect from their veterinarians. Every step of the way, clear, respectful, informed communication is emphasized with particular attention paid to shared medical decision-making.

The beautiful thing about the veterinarian-pet owner relationship is that there is always common ground. That common ground is right in front of us- whether purring, cuddling, chirping, barking, or slithering- but always looking at us with those eyes that make us want to be their best friend, their advocate.

Michael Cavanaugh, DVM
Executive Director
American Animal Hospital Association

66 He had as much fun in the water as any person I have known. You didn't have to throw a stick in the water to get him to go in. Of course, he would bring back a stick to you if you did throw one in. He would even have brought back a piano if you had thrown one in."

—JAMES THURBER

Introduction

I've been a veterinarian for just shy of three decades and still cannot imagine a profession I would enjoy more. The work has always been fulfilling, challenging, and exciting. When someone asks what kind of work I do, I'm always tickled by their delighted reaction when I tell them I am a vet. You'd be surprised how many times I'm told that they too wanted to become a veterinarian, but something managed to get in the way (usually organic chemistry). My kids have always received the same type of response when asked, "What does your mother do?" Just imagine how much easier it is for a kid to explain that Mom is a vet rather than an industry lobbyist or human resource specialist!

Historically, the veterinary profession has been almost unconditionally revered, that is, up until the last five to ten years. The way I perceive it is that "the James Herriot honeymoon" is now over. The perception that, simply because someone is a vet, he or she is wonderful is no longer universally embraced. Consumers of veterinary medicine have come to expect much, much more.

A 1999 survey* published in the *Journal of the American Veterinary Medical Association* (JAVMA) documented that people felt the most important and desirable attributes of a good veterinarian were kindness, gentleness, and respectfulness. Fast forward to 2008 when another survey of client expectations** published in JAVMA documented that it was no longer enough for a veterinarian to simply be a nice person. Far more important were the vet's willingness and ability to engage in two-way communication with her clients and

---

* JP Brown, et al, "The Current and Future Market for Veterinarians and Veterinary Services in the United States," *Journal of the American Veterinary Medical Association* 2:215 (1999): 15.161-183

** Jason B. Coe, et al, "A Focus Group Study of Veterinarians' and Pet Owners' Perceptions of Veterinarian-Client Communication in Companion Animal Medicine," *Journal of the American Veterinary Medical Association* 7:233 (2008): 10.1072-1080

deliver lots of information. Also considered important were use of understandable language (as opposed to medical-speak), discussion of all options regardless of cost, respect for the client's ultimate decision, and the ability of the vet to ask all the "right questions" pertaining to the animal's health as well as their role within the family.

I endearingly refer to the last decade as "The Coming of Age of the Empowered Client." What has created such change? Unquestionably, it coincides with mainstream use of the World Wide Web. The Internet has created savvy consumers of veterinary medicine with access to copious volumes of canine health information. No longer do my clients simply describe their dog's symptoms. They also provide me with Dr. Google's opinion about what may be causing the symptoms. And when I render a diagnosis, within minutes my clients can go on line and communicate with dozens of others who have "been there, done that" and are more than happy to provide advice and emotional support.

Do I believe such Internet-driven empowerment and changing client expectations are good things? You betcha! It's ideal when people want to be active, informed members of their dog's health care team. After all, no one knows their dogs better than they do. Their active voices are far more likely to result in choices that best serve the well being of their pets. Additionally, clients who are informed and involved tend to experience greater long-term peace of mind, whatever the medical outcome. Better medical decisions made for my patients and greater peace of mind for my clients- what could be better? There is one caveat to my unbridled enthusiasm about this state of empowerment. In order to avoid doing more harm than good, clients must learn to be responsible, discriminating Internet surfers (more about this in chapter nine).

Do you want your dog's doctor to be smart as a whip, an incredible surgeon, and a brilliant diagnostician? Of course you do! You are already familiar with such expectations when it comes to delivery of health care for members of your menagerie. The purpose of this book is to teach you about some other expectations you may not know about, but to which you are entitled. I want to help you become informed and involved, and receive the best possible health care for that amazing dog with whom you share your home and your heart.

Please know that I believe that each and every one of the expectations described in this book is truly reasonable. You should also know that veterinarians are not required to comply with them.

In fact, it may be difficult for some vets to "embrace" their clients' changing expectations. If you find this to be the case, I encourage you to try some gentle, respectful, persistent conversation with your veterinarian. If your vet isn't budging in response to your nudging, for your dog's sake, I encourage you to think about finding a new teammate. Concerned that you might hurt your veterinarian's feelings? I understand why you might feel this way, but please consider this question (which will be repeated more than once throughout this book): What is more important, your dog's health or your veterinarian's feelings?

If you find yourself in the position of looking for a veterinarian who is a better fit, I strongly encourage you to read the chapter called "Finding Dr. Wonderful and Your Mutt's Mayo Clinic" in *Speaking for Spot: Be the Advocate Your Dog Needs to Live a Happy, Healthy, Longer Life* (www.speakingforspot.com).

Note to the Reader

Unlike human medical doctors who need to think only in terms of their "patients," we in the veterinary profession are doubly blessed with "clients" and "patients." The "patient" is the cuddly creature before us, and the "client" refers to the human at the other end of the leash.

For the sake of my writing sanity and your reading sanity, I've made some gender decisions. Throughout this book, I've chosen to stick with the female gender when referring to veterinarians (best get used to this; at the time of publication more than eighty percent of veterinary school graduates within the United States are women). Female pronouns are also used when referring to clients. This leaves the male gender for the dogs who grace the pages of this book (no worries, given that there is no discussion about pregnancy or spaying).

For purposes of veterinary licensure, the terms "office," "clinic," and "hospital" have specific meanings. I am not following such convention and use these terms interchangeably throughout the following pages.

Just as I did in *Speaking for Spot*, throughout this book I have purposefully avoided the use of the term "dog owner." "Ownership" of a living, breathing creature with whom one shares an emotional relationship simply doesn't jive with the way I feel comfortable using the English language.

Whether you are a fan of Western (traditional, allopathic) medicine, Eastern (complementary, alternative) medicine, or prefer a combination of both, the reasonable expectations described herein will apply. Whichever style of medicine is preferred, shared decision-making between veterinarians and their clients is of great importance. This book is bound to be most helpful to those who embrace this philosophy. I fully recognize that shared decision-making is not for everyone. For some, peace of mind is better served by deferring the responsibility of making decisions solely to the veterinarian. I fully respect and acknowledge such differences.

" It came to me that every time I lose a dog they take a piece of my heart with them. And every new dog who comes into my life gifts me with a piece of their heart. If I live long enough, all the components of my heart will be dog, and I will become as generous and loving as they are."

—ANONYMOUS

Relationship Centered Care

I n the world of human medicine two major styles of communication exist between physicians and their patients. They are referred to as "relationship centered care" and "paternalistic care." The same terms can be applied to communication styles between veterinarians and their clients.

It is perfectly reasonable to expect relationship centered care from your veterinarian. Relationship centered care happens to be my "pet expectation" (pun intended) because, once fulfilled, satisfaction of all of the other expectations within the pages of this book will more naturally follow. Here is some information to help you understand the differences between relationship centered and paternalistic care.

Veterinarians who practice relationship centered care hold their clients' opinions and feelings in high regard, and allow enough time during the course of an office visit or telephone conversation to hear them. They learn about the special role their patients play in the lives of their human families and acknowledge the level of emotional attachment. Vets who practice relationship centered care recognize that their responsibilities expand beyond their patients to include the emotional well being of their clients. They are willing to be a source of empathy and support. Vets who are oriented towards relationship centered care believe in collaborative decision-making. Rather than *telling* their clients what to do, they make recommendations, and then ask for feedback, questions, and concerns.

Veterinarians who communicate paternalistically tend to dominate the office visit interaction, providing little opportunity for client questions, discussion or collaboration. Paternalistic care providers purposefully maintain an emotional distance from their clients. They accomplish this by conveying little to no interest in their clients' feelings or their special relationships with their dogs. They provide their medical recommendations based on what *they* believe is best for the patient without consideration of their clients' knowledge, experience, or feelings. Listen carefully for sentence starters such as, "If I were you I would……," "You need to……," "You have to…..," or "You should…….." Each phrase is a sure tip off that you are working with a veterinarian who communicates paternalistically.

I acknowledge that relationship centered care is not for everyone. Some people prefer that the professional involved be the decision maker (certainly the way I feel when my car is in need of repair). However, if you prefer relationship centered care from your vet (or for that matter, your own physician), you owe it to yourself to settle for nothing else. Need some advice on finding such a veterinarian? I encourage you to read "Finding Dr. Wonderful and Your Mutt's Mayo Clinic" in *Speaking for Spot*.

" An animal's eyes have the power to speak a great language."

—MARTIN BUBER

Round-the-Clock Care

If your dog is sick enough to require hospitalization or has just undergone a major surgical procedure, how will he be cared for throughout the night? As much as the mere thought of this makes me cringe, I must advise you that although you may be told your dog is being "hospitalized," in some veterinary clinics overnight hospitalization involves no supervision whatsoever from closing time at night until early the next morning when staff members return to work. What if your dog manages to slip out of his Elizabethan collar and chews open his surgical incision? What if he is experiencing pain? What if your best buddy vomits and then aspirates the material into his lungs? All these "what ifs" are what make me crazy whenever I think about a hospitalized patient left alone for hours at a time, be it overnight or during the weekend.

Know that it is perfectly reasonable for you to expect your hospitalized dog to receive round-the-clock care. Unless "hospitalization" is clearly defined by a staff member, you *must* ask for clarification. (If courage doesn't happen to be your strong suit, remind yourself that your dog really needs you to be his medical advocate.)

Options for 24-Hour Care

Transfer to a 24-Hour Care Hospital: Many emergency and specialty hospitals offer round-the-clock patient monitoring as a service to local veterinarians. If your veterinarian cannot provide such supervision herself, she may recommend transfer to a 24-hour care facility. While 24-hour hospitals staffed with veterinarians and technicians are ideal, such facilities simply do not exist in all communities. If one is present in your neck of the woods, by all means take advantage! Here are some other viable options for round-the-clock care, any of which are much better than leaving your ailing dog alone and unsupervised:

Veterinarian Observation: A vet comes into the clinic multiple times throughout the night to check on hospitalized patients. Some docs prefer to take their patients home with them overnight or over the weekend to make monitoring and supervision more convenient.

Technician Observation: A skilled veterinary technician comes into the clinic multiple times throughout the night to check on hospitalized patients and has ready access to the veterinarian should questions or concerns arise.

Home Observation: Your dog spends the night at home with you, but only after you receive *thorough* monitoring instructions along with a way to reach your vet or an experienced technician should questions or concerns arise. As scary as this may seem, this remains a better option than leaving your sweetie pie completely unsupervised. Just imagine how you would feel lying in a hospital bed, hooked up to intravenous fluids, with no one entering your room to check on you for twelve or more long hours!

Until one has loved an animal, a part of one's soul remains unawakened."

—ANATOLE FRANCE

❸

Access to "The Back" of the Hospital

Care to tag along the next time your dog is whisked to "the back" of the hospital for an injection, a diagnostic test, or a nail trim? Perhaps you are curious about what actually goes on "back" there. Maybe you believe that your best buddy will feel more secure if you are present. Whatever the reason, know that if you have the desire to go where your dog goes and see what your dog sees, this is a perfectly reasonable expectation in *most* circumstances.

I happen to like having my clients observe what my technicians and I are doing. In fact, in many ways it makes our jobs easier for the following reasons:

☛ The client who gets a first-hand look at the abnormality I am seeing under the microscope or on the ultrasound screen often gains a clearer understanding of the next-step options, more so than had she only received my after-the-fact verbal description.

☛ The client who observes her sweet little "Dr. Jekyll" transform into formidable "Mr. Hyde" in response to restraint for cleaning ears or shooting an x-ray, more clearly understands why sedation is necessary to get the job done in an effective, safe, and humane fashion.

☛ The client who observes a clean, well-maintained facility with a bustling staff, content and comfortable patients in clean comfy cages, and state-of-the-art diagnostic and patient monitoring equipment better understands why the cost of veterinary medicine is what it is today!

☛ For some nervous patients, having their best friend by their side can be a calming source of comfort.

Why You Might Hear, "No"

While I believe it is perfectly reasonable for you to expect access to the back of the hospital, know that not all veterinarians feel as I do.

Their reasoning is based on what they believe works best for their patients and staff efficiency. Here are some potential reasons why your expectation to tag along might be deemed unreasonable:

- Your dog is better behaved *without* you there. All vets have witnessed patients who are aggressive in the exam room, but become gentle as lambs when separated from their humans.

- There is something happening in the back of the hospital that is too private (for example, a grieving client) or too graphic (trust your vet on this one) for you to see.

- Your dog will be in an area of the hospital that is off limits to you. For example, at the time of publication, in California, no one other than the patient is allowed in the room when an x-ray is taken (this is meant to be a human health safeguard). Gentle sand bags are used for restraint along with mild sedation if needed. The operating room is another site that is typically off limits for fear of compromising sterility of the surgical procedure.

- The staff feels that you may be in harm's way. Every single staff member feels horrible if a client is bitten, scratched, or injured in some way while trying to care for the patient. And when a client is injured, the owner of the facility may be legally liable.

☛ Staff members may feel nervous or anxious performing procedures such as drawing a blood sample or placing an intravenous catheter under the watchful eye of the client. As you might imagine, nerves have the potential to sabotage the success of the task at hand.

☛ Staff members are aware that you have a lot to say and they will not be able to get their work done because they will be too busy responding to your questions and comments.

What You Can Do

If accompanying your dog to the back of the hospital is a priority for you, but your request is met with resistance, I encourage you to try some gentle persuasion. Provide reassurance that you will be on your best behavior (you will be unobtrusive and will avoid asking a bazillion questions). Remind the reluctant staff member that large animal docs do practically all of their work in front of their clients. Lastly, if you receive a negative response to your request to tag along, make sure the response is coming from the "boss" and not from an employee who happens to be feeling overworked and underappreciated at the time of your request.

By the way, accompanying your dog into the back of the hospital is not for everyone. Some clients prefer to run an errand or hang out in the waiting room while their dog is being cared for. Some folks are downright squeamish, and before I ask a client to accompany me into "the bowels" of the hospital I provide a graphic description of what they will be seeing. This deters some, and that is a good thing- nothing like a fainting or vomiting client to get the day off to an exciting start!

" There is no psychiatrist in the world like a puppy licking your face."

—BEN WILLIAMS

Discussion of all Options Regardless of Cost

Veterinarians wear many different hats when they enter an exam room. It's a given that they provide health care for their patients. But did you know that, on an as needed basis, vets also assume the role of social worker, calendar planner, grief counselor, and conflict mediator (particularly when spouses are at odds with one another)? It is no wonder we are always running behind schedule! Vets are willing to do all of this because they know their efforts directly benefit their patient's health and/or their client's peace of mind.

Some veterinarians also assume the misguided responsibility of acting as their client's "financial planner." They do so by picking and choosing which medical and surgical options to discuss based on what they *think* their clients can afford. Their perceptions may be based on past experience with the individual as well as the client's demeanor, appearance, and/or source of employment (or lack thereof).

Please know that it is one hundred percent reasonable for you to expect your veterinarian to advise you of every option that makes medical sense for your dog, regardless of cost. It is unacceptable for her to withhold discussion of certain options based on perceived affordability. What an individual is willing to spend to care for their dog's health is unpredictable at best. A client who arrives in a luxury sports sedan may decline recommended care because veterinary expenditures don't jive with her spending values. Another client who works full time to feed her family might choose to take on a second job in order to finance the hope of improving her dog's health.

Purposefully withholding discussion of all reasonable options based on perceived affordability can be damaging, both in terms of the patient's health as well as the psychological well being of the human at the other end of the leash. When someone learns that a better option was not discussed, particularly if her dog's health declines or he passes away, the emotional price can be devastating. Under such circumstances it is not uncommon for people to become mired in the grief process, experiencing prolonged and profound anger, sadness, and/or guilt.

For your own sake, and for your dog's sake, I encourage you to let your veterinarian know up front that you would like to hear about *every* option pertaining to your dog's health care, regardless of cost. This is a perfectly reasonable expectation!

66 When you adopt a dog, the whole experience is fraught with delightful unpredictability. Very little is certain~except, of course, that you will be giving him a better life. And he will be doing the same for you."

—PETER MAYLE

5

Written Cost Estimates

You've just taken your dog to the vet because he's been vomiting for three days and now he's refusing his food. Your vet performs a thorough physical examination, but finds nothing out of the ordinary. She recommends some blood tests along with x-rays of your dog's belly. If the diagnosis remains uncertain, the next recommended step will be abdominal ultrasound. You give your vet the green light to proceed with testing. After all, your dog is a beloved family member and you want him to get well. But, do you know how much all of this diagnostic testing will cost? Will you be charged $300, $800, or $1,300? Unless your dog is a "repeat offender" and you've been to your vet clinic way too many times, how in the world could you possibly know what the cost will be? Three hundred dollars might be completely within your budget, whereas $1,300 might mean coming up short on your mortgage payment.

Requesting a Cost Estimate

Whether you are independently wealthy, barely making ends meet, or somewhere in between, know that it is perfectly reasonable to receive a written cost estimate from your veterinarian *before* services are provided. You may need to initiate this request because many vets are not in the habit of automatically providing written cost estimates. This is supported by research published within the Journal of the American Veterinary Medical Association. The paper[*] titled, "Prevalence and Nature of Cost Discussions During Clinical Appointments in Companion Animal Practice" documented the following:

- ☛ The actual cost of services provided is addressed during only 29% of veterinary appointments.

---

[*] Jason B. Coe, et al, "Prevalence and Nature of Cost Discussions During Clinical Appointments in Companion Animal Practice," Journal of the American Veterinary Medical Association 1;234 (2009): 11.1418-1424

- When fees are discussed, 33% of the time the discussion is initiated by the client rather than the veterinarian.
- Conversation related to cost information constitutes a mere 4.3% of the total dialogue time between veterinarian and client.
- Written cost estimates are discussed during only 14% of appointments.
- Written cost estimates are actually prepared and delivered to the client in only 8% of appointments.

This data suggests that many veterinarians are a bit squeamish when it comes to discussing their fees. Talking about a dog's health is one thing. Discussing financial matters is a whole 'nother ball game! That being said, an up front conversation about estimated fees is far more comfortable than back peddling with a client who is feeling shocked, overwhelmed, or angry because of the total on her invoice.

Written Versus Verbal Cost Estimates

I strongly encourage you to request a written rather than a verbal cost estimate. (Don't encourage your vet to simply give you a "ballpark" estimate or one "off the top of her head.") Written estimates are far more likely to be accurate than those prepared by a veterinarian performing mental math while on the fly. Additionally, written estimates avoid any uncomfortable "he said, she said" conversations.

I avoid providing guesstimates to my clients at all costs (pun intended). Try as I might, I invariably lowball such verbal estimates because of my innate desire to make my services more affordable. Once a client has a lowball estimate, I may end up having to cut a few corners (never a good thing for the patient) and/or making uncomfortable phone calls to advise clients of added expenses. And I definitely get called into the principal's (my hospital administrator's) office!

With written estimates everybody wins. Communication is so much cleaner and clearer, and there are no surprises when it comes time to collect fees. Additionally, a written cost estimate provides an itemization of everything that is planned for your pooch, always a good thing to know.

❝ No man can be condemned for owning a dog. As long as he has a dog, he has a friend; and the poorer he gets, the better friend he has."

—WILL ROGERS

Referral for Second Opinions and Specialized Care

In human medicine, a second opinion results in a new diagnosis as often as thirty percent of the time. There are no such statistics available in veterinary medicine, but as an internist who provides a lot of second opinions, I have every reason to believe that the percentage is comparable. The clearest benefit of a second opinion is for your dog. Although the health outcome may not be a positive one, another point of view often facilitates a more expedient diagnosis and treatment plan. The other beneficiary of a second opinion is you! Second opinions provide reassurance, and allow you to feel more confident that you are doing the best thing possible for that dog you love so dearly.

A Second Opinion is Always Okay

It is perfectly reasonable to expect your veterinarian to support referral for a second opinion. She may be the one to suggest that another vet have a look, or it may be up to you to broach this topic. Either way, a second opinion makes good sense in any of the following circumstances:

- ☛ You want more certainty about a diagnosis.
- ☛ You want more certainty about a recommended diagnostic test, procedure, or treatment plan.
- ☛ A number of tests have been run without yielding a clear-cut diagnosis.
- ☛ Your vet has recommended a complicated surgery or other significant procedure.
- ☛ Your dog isn't getting any better or is getting worse in response to what you and your veterinarian have been trying.
- ☛ You want more information about alternative treatment options.

☛ Your vet doesn't specialize in the disease your dog has or the treatment he needs.

☛ You've lost faith in your veterinarian.

☛ You simply have a gut feeling that a second opinion makes sense.

What You Will Need

In preparation for a second opinion appointment, your veterinary staff will ideally supply you with copies of your dog's medical record including all laboratory data, x-rays, EKG (electrocardiogram) recordings, and ultrasound report and images. A case summary letter written by your veterinarian is always tremendously helpful. Without these things in hand, the second opinion appointment won't be as productive, or tests will need to be repeated (an unnecessary hardship for your dog and your bank account).

Referral to a Specialist

Veterinary technology has advanced by leaps and bounds over the past couple of decades. From MRI scans to cancer vaccines to stem cell therapy, there simply is no way an individual veterinarian can be proficient at everything. The number of veterinary specialists is growing rapidly as more and more vet school graduates choose to advance their knowledge in a specific area of expertise. Much like Starbucks®, if there's not already a group of specialists in your neighborhood, there likely will be soon!

Veterinarians cannot become specialists simply because they have an interest or aptitude in a particular field. The term "specialist" is reserved for those with the desire (and fortitude) to have continued their education beyond four years of veterinary school. They must also complete a minimum three-year internship and residency training program, author publications, and then pass rigorous specialty examinations. The culmination of this extended, specialized training and testing is referred to as "board certification." Qualifications required to achieve "certification," the term applied to specialization in complementary/alternative medicine (Chinese herbs, acupuncture, chiropractic, homeopathy, rehabilitation) vary depending on the treatment modality. See page 38 for a listing of the different specialists and their associated organizations. You may find specialists in your area by visiting the listed organization websites.

It is perfectly reasonable to expect that your vet will contact a specialist to discuss your dog when advice is needed. She may refer you to a specialist for a second opinion or when specialty diagnostic testing or treatment is warranted. Chances are, your veterinarian has established good working relationships with a variety of specialists in your area. As is the case for second opinions, your vet may initiate referral to a specialist or it may be up to you to recognize when consultation with a specialist makes sense.

Discussing Second Opinions and Referral to Specialists

If you feel a bit sheepish about initiating a conversation with your veterinarian regarding a second opinion or referral to a specialist, know that you are not alone. If you need a bit of help getting the ball rolling, you'll find some easy and nonthreatening "conversation starters" in chapter number nine of *Speaking for Spot*. Many people worry about hurting their vet's feelings. Keep in mind, your veterinarian is a big girl! If her feelings should be a little bit hurt, though it is unlikely they will be, she will get over it. Unless she's fresh out of vet school, this won't be the first time a client requested a second opinion or referral to a specialist and it won't be the last. Remember, your vet's primary concern should be your dog's health- not her own feelings!

Veterinary Specialty Organizations

Organization	Specialty	Designation
American College of Veterinary Small Animal Internal Medicine (www.acvim.org)	Internal medicine	Diplomate, ACVIM
American College of Veterinary Internal Medicine, Cardiology (www.acvim.org)	Cardiology	Diplomate, ACVIM, cardiology
American College of Veterinary Internal Medicine, Neurology (www.acvim.org)	Neurology	Diplomate, ACVIM, neurology
American College of Veterinary Internal Medicine, Oncology (www.acvim.org)	Oncology (cancer medicine)	Diplomate, ACVIM, oncology
American College of Veterinary Surgeons (www.acvs.org)	Surgery	Diplomate, ACVS
American College of Veterinary Dermatology (www.acvd.org)	Dermatology	Diplomate, ACVD
American College of Veterinary Radiology (www.acvr.org)	Radiology	Diplomate, ACVR
American College of Veterinary Ophthalmology (www.acvo.org)	Ophthalmology	Diplomate, ACVO
American College of Veterinary Emergency and Critical Care (www.acvecc.org)	Emergency and critical care	Diplomate, AVECC
American College of Veterinary Anesthesiologists (www.acva.org)	Anesthesiology	Diplomate, ACVA
American College of Veterinary Behaviorists (www.dacvb.org)	Behavior	Diplomate, DACVB
American College of Veterinary Nutrition (www.acvn.org)	Nutrition	Diplomate, ACVN
American Veterinary Dental College (www.avdc.org)	Dentistry	Diplomate, AVDC
American College of Theriogenologists (www.theriogenology.org)	Theriogenology (reproductive medicine)	Diplomate, ACT
American Board of Veterinary Practitioners (www.abvp.com)	General practice	Diplomate, ABVP

QUICK REFERENCE
Veterinary Specialty Organizations

Organization	Specialty	Abbreviation
International Veterinary Acupuncture Society (www.ivas.org)	Veterinary acupuncture	CVA
International Veterinary Academy of Pain Management (www.ivapm.org)	Pain Management	CVPP
Chi Institute (www.tcvm.com) (acupuncture and Chinese herb therapy)	Chinese veterinary medicine	TCVM
Academy of Veterinary Homeopathy (www.theavh.org)	Homeopathy	AVH
Professional Course in Veterinary Homeopathy (www.drpitcairn.com)	Homeopathy	AVH
Animal Chiropractic Certification Commission (www.animalchiropractic.org)	Chiropractic	AVCA
University of Tennessee Certificate Program in Canine Physical Rehabilitation (www.canineequinerehab.com)	Canine rehabilitation therapy	CCRP (CCRT CCRA)
Canine Rehabilitation Institute (www.caninerehabinstitute.com)	Canine rehabilitation therapy	CCRP (CCRT CCRA)

❝ You can say any foolish thing to a dog, and the dog will give you a look that says, "My God you're right! I never would've thought of that!'"

—DAVE BARRY

Discussion About Your Dog's Vaccinations

When I graduated from veterinary school in 1982 there were five canine vaccines to choose from. We vaccinated every dog with "the works" once a year, no questions asked. My, oh my, how things have changed! Nowadays, the world of canine vaccines is a constantly shifting landscape, and it is no longer in your dog's best interest to vaccinate for everything simply because you've received a reminder postcard or email.

It is perfectly reasonable (imperative, in my opinion) for you to expect a thorough discussion with your vet about your dog's vaccinations before they are administered. Determining the best protocol (when to vaccinate, which diseases to vaccinate against, how many vaccines to administer at one time) requires a case-by-case assessment that involves input from both you and your vet. Beyond the puppy series of immunizations for distemper, parvovirus, and rabies, there is no "one size fits all" protocol.

American Animal Hospital Association Guidelines

Because of the growing complexity surrounding canine vaccines, the American Animal Hospital Association (AAHA) organized a task force in 2003 to develop a set of standard vaccination guidelines for veterinarians. The task force reconvened in 2006, and again in 2011 to update their work. AAHA defines vaccination as "a medical procedure with definite benefits and risks, and one that should be undertaken only with individualization of vaccine choices and after input from the client." Keep in mind that the AAHA task force has provided recommendations only. Veterinarians are not required to abide by these guidelines.

Consider the Following

- At the time of publication, vaccinations are available to provide protection against more than a dozen different canine diseases.

- The duration and degree of immunity (protection) provided by any vaccine vary not only by manufacturer, but from dog to dog as well.

- It is now recognized that distemper and parvovirus vaccines, once routinely given annually, provide protection from disease for a minimum of three years. In fact, for some dogs the protection is life-long.

- Other than for rabies (state mandated), vaccination protocols are anything but standardized. There are no set rules that must be followed when determining which vaccines to give, how many are given at one time, and how often they are administered. Some vets give multiple inoculations at once, others administer just one at a time. Some vets continue to vaccinate for distemper and parvovirus annually while many others have transitioned to the more appropriate protocol (once every three years).

- Increasingly clear-cut documentation shows that vaccines have the potential to cause many side effects. On occasion, adverse vaccine reactions are life threatening. Administering multiple vaccines at the same time is associated with an increased risk of adverse reactions, particularly in small breed dogs.

Things to Discuss With Your Veterinarian

As you now realize, there's a good deal to discuss with your veterinarian *before* your dog is vaccinated. I encourage you to include all of the following topics:

1. Discuss your dog's "biolifestyle" (what diseases he may be exposed to based on where you live and your dog's extracurricular activities). For example, if your best buddy frequents a boarding kennel, the kennel cough vaccination (Bordatella and Parainfluenza) makes good sense. If you live in rattlesnake country and your dog happens to be a Jack Russell Terrier (the breed least likely to back away from a rattlesnake encounter), you and your vet will want to discuss the rattlesnake vaccine. Conversely, if your little princess resides in a Manhattan penthouse, there is no benefit, only risk to be gained from vaccinating to protect against Lyme disease (spread by ticks).

2. Alert your veterinarian to any symptoms or medical issues your

dog is experiencing. It is almost always best to avoid vaccinating a dog who is sick – better to let his immune system concentrate on getting rid of the current illness rather than creating a vaccine "distraction." If your dog has a history of autoimmune (immune-mediated) disease, it may be advisable to alter his vaccine protocol or even forego ongoing vaccinations because of the potential for inoculations to trigger disease recurrence. In such cases, performing vaccine titers (serology) can help make a sound decision about whether or not to vaccinate (see number 4 below).

3. Be sure to let your vet know if your dog has had any vaccine side effects in the past, even if the symptoms appeared only mild. In response, she may choose to use a vaccine product from a different manufacturer, avoid giving multiple vaccinations all at once, and/or pre-treat with medication to prevent side effects. If the adverse reaction to a previous vaccine was serious enough, she may recommend that future vaccinations be discontinued.

4. If vaccine serology (titer testing) is of interest to you, discuss this topic with your veterinarian. Serology involves testing your dog's blood (requiring only a small sample) to determine if adequate vaccine protection against canine distemper and/or parvo-

virus is present. While such testing isn't perfect, in general if the blood test result indicates active and adequate protection, a vaccine booster can be postponed, or serology can be repeated in the future. Serologic testing for your dog may make better sense than simply vaccinating at set intervals. Titer testing can also be used to ensure adequate vaccine protection following completion of puppy immunizations.

5. Discuss the potential side effects of proposed vaccinations, what you should be watching for, and whether or not there are any restrictions for your dog in the days immediately following his inoculations. Together with your vet, determine if it's best to give multiple vaccinations all at once or spread out over time.

6. What should you do if your veterinarian declines vaccine discussion and simply wants to vaccinate your dog based on what he or she thinks is appropriate? Time to find yourself a new vet who embraces a more progressive style of practice and enjoys working with people who want to be involved in their dog's health care.

Learning More

How can you learn more about vaccination protocols and the best choices for your dog? In addition to the information provided below, I encourage you to read the chapter called, "The Vaccination Conundrum" in *Speaking for Spot* as well the most recently updated version of the the AAHA vaccine guidelines (https://www.aahanet.org/library/Guidelines.aspx).

The Importance of Annual Examinations

Please allow me a paragraph to get on my soapbox. Our recognition that adult distemper and parvovirus vaccine protection lasts a minimum of three years has been of great benefit in terms of avoiding the risks associated with over-vaccinating. Unfortunately, there has also been a downside to our newer understanding about vaccines. You see, historically we've done too good a job with those vaccine reminder postcards and emails. We have inadvertently programmed some folks to believe that vaccinations are the most, if not the only important part of their dog's regular visits to the vet clinic. Nothing could be further from the truth, yet, at the time of publication, many dogs visit the vet and receive a thorough physical examination just once every three years (timed with their vaccinations) rather than annually. As you might imagine, veterinarians are concerned about losing the opportunity for early disease detection and treatment for their patients. It's a no-brainer that the earlier cancer is detected, the better the outcome. The same is true for heart disease, kidney disease, periodontal disease, and a myriad of other medical issues that might be discovered during a routine physical examination. The annual office visit also provides time to discuss nutrition, behavioral issues, parasite control, and anything else that warrants veterinary advice. I strongly encourage you to commit to an annual vet visit (even more frequently if your dog is a senior citizen) for your best buddy. Besides, won't it be nice for your dog to see the vet and receive lots of attention and treats without the shots!

" One of the happiest sights in the world comes when a lost dog is reunited with a master he loves. You just haven't seen joy till you have seen that."

—ELDON ROARK

Discussion About Your Dog's Diet

Do you remember a time when pet stores had only one dog food aisle? Nowadays, a dozen aisles wouldn't be enough to display the myriad of available diets. New products hit the market every day as pet food manufacturers vie for your dog's grocery money. You can choose a food based on your dog's breed, size, life stage, or fitness level. There are diets designed for disease prevention and others designed for treatment of disease. Your dog no longer needs to eat plain ole' beef, pork or chicken for dinner. These days, fish, venison, rabbit, duck, and even kangaroo are the primary ingredients in an array of novel protein diets for pooches with sensitive stomachs. Care to feed your dog a low fat, low protein, or low carbohydrate food? You'll have no trouble finding such products. And if all of these options weren't enough, you also have the choice of purchasing food for your dog that is raw or processed (canned food or kibble). Lastly, if so inclined, you can skip the dog food aisle altogether and prepare Fido's feast at home. So many choices can make the decision of "what to feed my dog" rather mind boggling, quite honestly, even for a veterinarian!

What your dog eats is an important element of his health care, so discussing his diet with your veterinarian makes perfect sense. What can be a bit tricky is having an *open-minded* discussion, one in which both you and your vet are willing to hear each other's preferences and biases. These days, it's not uncommon for people to have strong opinions when discussing what should and shouldn't go into a dog's stomach. Talk with folks who work with dogs (trainers, groomers, breeders, veterinary staff members) and you just might get an earful of conflicting "diet dogma" (pun intended) such as:

- ☛ Processed diets are the best way to ensure balanced nutrition.
- ☛ Processed diets are the devil incarnate.
- ☛ Home-cooked diets are the best way to feed a pet.

- Home-cooked diets are not nutritionally balanced.

- Raw diets promote the best health.

- Raw diets transmit serious infectious diseases to dogs and their humans.

- Dogs should eat the same food every day.

- Dogs should eat a variety of foods.

At the time of publication, there is very little scientific evidence that supports or refutes any of the above claims. Yet, many veterinarians are adamantly at odds with one another about what their canine patients should be eating. Perhaps future research will be enlightening, but until that time, I simply don't buy into the notion that there is only one right way to feed a dog.

When you discuss diet choices with your veterinarian I encourage you to stay focused on your common ground, namely your best buddy. Your mutual top priority is his health and well-being. No doubt, you both can agree that your dog should be eating food that contains high quality ingredients and is nutritionally balanced. Hear what your veterinarian's dietary recommendations are, based on your dog's age, breed, and lifestyle. Your dog's health issues may steer your vet towards a particular diet or type of food. Likewise, hopefully your vet will hear what you have to say about diet preferences and what type of product (kibble, canned food, raw food, homemade diet) you feel most comfortable feeding. The goal is to work together to come up with options that allow both you and your vet to feel okay with the choice that is made. Of course, your dog is really the one with the final choice when he decides whether or not the food in his bowl is worthy of eating!

“ She has no particular breed in mind, no unusual requirements, except the special sense of mutual recognition that tells dog and human they have both come to the right place.”

—LLOYD ALEXANDER

Discussion About Your Internet Research

When your dog develops a medical issue, chances are you'll do some Internet research, and it's only natural that you would wish to talk with your veterinarian about what you've learned. I happen to enjoy hearing what my clients are discovering online. I sometimes come away with valuable new information, and I'm invariably amused by the extraordinary things they tell me. (Who knew that hip dysplasia is caused by global warming!)

Surf to your heart's content, but be forewarned, not all veterinarians feel as I do. Some have a hard time not "rolling their eyes" or quickly interrupting the moment the conversation turns to Internet research.

Who can blame them? They've grown weary of spending valuable office visit, telephone, or email time talking their clients out of the wackadoodle notions they've gleaned from cyberspace and reining them in from online wild goose chases.

Responsible Internet Surfing

Whether veterinarians like it or not, the Internet is here to stay. What can you do to make discussions with your vet regarding your online research more valuable? Presented below are some tips to help you differentiate instructive, accurate, credible Internet information from "online junk food." By the way, although I'm a veterinarian teaching people how to better care for their dogs, much of this information is also applicable to your own healthcare!

☛ Ask your veterinarian for her website recommendations, those that have already been "vetted."

☛ Veterinary college websites invariably provide reliable information. Search for them by entering "veterinary college" or "veterinary school" after the name of the disease or symptom you are researching.

- Web addresses ending in ".edu," and ".gov" represent educational institutions and governmental agencies, respectively. Such sites will likely be sources of accurate information.

- If your dog has a breed-specific disease, pay a visit to the website hosted by the breed's national organization. Up to date information may appear here long before it makes its way into something your veterinarian might read. Within veterinary journals there can be a lag time of one to two years between submission of new information and publication.

- Avoid business-sponsored websites that stand to make money when you believe and act on what they profess. Be dubious of the information found on websites recommending purchase of a product.

- Be ever so wary of anecdotal information (stories told by individuals about their own experiences). It's perfectly okay to indulge yourself with remarkable tales (how Max's skin disease was miraculously cured by a single session of aromatherapy), but view what you are reading as fiction rather than fact. As fascinating as these *National Enquirer*-type stories may seem, please don't let them significantly influence the choices you make for your dog. As much as you may want to believe that the story about Max applies to your Sophie, it is unlikely that they have the same disease or would experience the same response to therapy.

☛ I'm a big fan of most disease-specific online forums. Not only do they provide a wealth of educational information, they also offer you a large community of people who are dealing with the same challenge as you. Forum members can be a wonderful source of emotional support- always a good thing for those of us who share our homes and our hearts with a dog.

Look for a forum that focuses on a specific disease (kidney failure, diabetes, etc.), has lots of members, and has been up and running for several years. A large group such as this typically has multiple moderators who provide more than one point of view (always a good thing) and greater round-the-clock availability for advice and support.

Look for cited references (clinical research that supports what is being recommended). Such groups should have a homepage that explains the focus of the group and provides the number of members and posts per month (the more the better). They may have public archives of previous posts that can provide a wealth of information.

Making your Internet Discussion Worthwhile

Now that you are adept at surfing the 'net, how can you comfortably discuss what you've learned with your veterinarian? I cannot overemphasize the importance of working with a vet who is happy and willing to participate in two-way, collaborative dialogue with you. A veterinarian who practices such relationship centered care is far more likely to be willing to hear about your online research than a vet who practices paternalistically (see chapter one). Remember, when it comes to veterinarian-client communication styles, you have a choice. It's up to you to make the right choice!

If you feel sheepish about discussing your Internet research for fear that, in doing so, you may convey a lack of faith in your veterinarian, I encourage you to get over it! Online research is commonplace these days and hearing about it should be part of every veterinarian's job description. Besides, what is more important, your dog's health or your veterinarian's feelings?

Here are some tips for having constructive and comfortable dialogue with your vet about what you have learned online:

- Wait for the appropriate time during the office visit to discuss what you've learned. Allow your veterinarian to ask questions of you and examine your dog rather than "tackling" her with your Internet research the moment she sets foot in the exam room.

- Let your vet know that you've learned to be a discriminating Internet surfer! You know how to differentiate between valuable online resources and "cyber-fluff." Also tell her that you appreciate her willingness and patience in helping you understand how to best utilize what you've learned online.

- Be brief and to the point with your questions. Remember, most veterinarians have only 15 to 20 minutes max to complete an office visit.

- When you initiate conversation about your Internet research, I encourage you to choose your words wisely. Communicate in a respectful fashion that invites conversation as opposed to "telling" your vet what you want to do based on what you've read.

In the Internet, we have an extraordinary tool at our fingertips, and discussing what you've learned with your veterinarian is a perfectly reasonable expectation. I encourage you to be critical when choosing which websites you intend to take seriously and which ones you wish to visit for a good chuckle. Approach conversations with your vet about your Internet research thoughtfully and tactfully. These strategies are bound to create a win-win-win situation, for you, your veterinarian, and your beloved best friend!

“ If a dog will not come to you after having looked you in the face, you should go home and examine your conscience."

—WOODROW WILSON

Communicating Via Email

Have you any interest in emailing your veterinarian when you have questions or concerns about your dog's health? While this is a reasonable expectation, know that not all vets are keen on this idea quite yet. Email communication with doctors is a relatively new concept. Kaiser Permanente, a human health maintenance organization (HMO) that is available in many parts of the United States has set an extremely positive precedent regarding the benefits of email communication between health care providers and their patients. Not only are more and more Kaiser Permanente patients emailing their doctors, a study of more than 30,000 patients with high blood pressure and/or diabetes documented that those who communicated with their physicians via email enjoyed better health outcomes.[*]

I surveyed 120 northern California small animal veterinarians (both general practitioners and specialists) in 2011 to learn about their use of email communication with clients. I must issue forth the following two disclaimers: First, at present, this is unpublished data. Second, who knows if those somewhat quirky vets practicing in northern California truly represent what goes on in the rest of the world! (It's okay, I can say this because I practiced there for 29 years.) Here is what I learned from my survey:

- 58% of the vets surveyed reported that they were communicating with their clients via email.

- 62% of those using email communication were selective about which of their clients were provided with email access.

- 26% of those using email communication established email "ground rules" for their clients. Interestingly, many of the vets using email communication with their clients commented that they felt a strong need to set ground rules, but were simply too "wimpy" to do so.

[*] Yi Yvonne Zhou, et al. "Improved Quality at Kaiser Permanente Through E-Mail Between Physicians and Patients," Health Affairs 10:1377 (2010): 29.1370-1375

☛ 95% of those using email communication reported it to be a mostly positive experience.

The Benefits of Email Communication

The veterinarians who responded to my survey reported that email is a wonderful tool for simple, non-urgent communications (emphasis on non-urgent). Imagine every veterinarian's worst nightmare- she checks her email in the evening and finds a message sent eight hours earlier from a client describing a dog with blue gums and struggling to breathe!

Many vets enjoy the convenience of email. Not only does it avoid "telephone tag," responses can be generated at any time, night or day. For me this is a huge plus as I may not finish up with my patients until 8:30 or 9:00 at night at which point I'm concerned that it might be too late for a phone call.

The Potential Pitfalls of Email Communication

Along with not receiving urgent messages in a timely fashion, the major email concerns expressed by the veterinarians surveyed included:

☛ Some clients want a diagnosis based on an email description or photo with hopes of avoiding an office visit.

☛ There is no simple way to transfer email communications from the computer into the patient's medical record.

☛ Email is too time consuming for vets who have remedial word processing skills or feel the need to carefully edit every written word.

☛ Some clients seem to take advantage of the system and email too much and too often.

☛ Some clients make it a habit to send "cutesy emails" (those photos or stories that are incredibly cute, in the mind of the sender, that is).

While your expectation to communicate with your veterinarian via email is perfectly reasonable, know that she may not be on board with this. Explore the idea with her and let her know you will comply with any and all ground rules. Even if your vet does not feel a need to create ground rules, I strongly encourage you to limit your email communication to non-urgent matters. Email offers a great way to ask uncomplicated questions and provide medical updates requested by your veterinarian. Remember, email is not instant messaging- it is not intended for back and forth conversation (at least not with your doggie's doctor).

When discussing anything other than simple matters with your veterinarian, it's important that she be able to know how you are feeling about things. She can best accomplish this by picking up on your voice inflections and/or body language, neither of which can be perceived via email. In this regard, email communication is never a good substitute for a face-to-face conversation or good old-fashioned telephone call. Who knows, when I revise this book in the future, perhaps I will discuss the reasonable expectation of Skyping with your vet!

" His head on my knee can heal my human hurts. His presence by my side is protection against my fears of dark and unknown things. He has promised to wait for me... whenever... wherever, in case I need him. And I expect I will, as I always have. He is just my dog."

—GENE HILL

Visiting Your Dog While He Is Hospitalized

There are two important reasons to visit your best buddy while he is in the hospital. While there are no studies proving that hospitalized dogs derive significant benefit from getting to spend time with their favorite humans, I certainly believe it is true. In fact, I like to include visits from home as part of every patient's treatment plan with hopes of hastening their recovery. Such "psychological chicken soup" may be exactly what the dog needs and, as the saying goes, "It couldn't hurt!"

In addition to providing benefit for your dog, visiting him while he is hospitalized may provide you with some important peace of mind. Perhaps the two of you have never spent a night apart, or you are worried that he is distressed or in pain. You will benefit from seeing him on a nice comfy blanket attended to by competent, caring staff members. Furthermore, spending some nose-to-nose time with your sweetie pie will give you a better sense of his health status and whether or not it is changing. Your veterinarian's impression of your dog's progress might even change based on your visit. This is because some hospitalized patients who appear depressed and uninterested in eating food instantly perk up and chow down when the people they adore are present.

Know that it is perfectly reasonable for you to expect to visit your dog while he is in the hospital. It's not always easy to think straight with a sick or injured dog on your hands, but I strongly encourage you to ask about the hospital visitation policy *before* your dog is admitted. If visits are not allowed, it's pretty darned clear that you and your dog are in the wrong place. Unless it would be detrimental to his health, I encourage you to consider moving your dog to another hospital for ongoing care.

Visitation Policies

When visiting your dog be sure to abide by the hospital's policies. There may be specific visiting hours and/or limits on how long you can stay. Don't take your dog out for a walk, offer water, or bring his favorite treats from home without first asking (your vet may be purposefully withholding such amenities). Do your best to avoid distracting the technicians as they care for your dog and other hospitalized patients, although expressions of gratitude are always welcome. Lastly, tempted as you may be to interact with all of the patients, best to keep your attention (and your hands) focused on your own beloved pet!

When Not to Visit

On occasion, family visits for a hospitalized dog are contraindicated (they have the potential to cause more harm than good). For example, your veterinarian may prefer that her patient remain sound asleep for the first 12 to 24 hours following major surgery. Just imagine how the excitement of seeing Mom or Dad might disrupt this plan! Some hospitalized dogs experience a prolonged period of overexcitement or depression once a visit from home has ended. I suspect these dogs are thinking, "I cannot believe she left me here again!" Fortunately, this behavior is the exception rather than the rule. It is difficult, however to predict which dogs are going to react this way. If your dog is hospitalized be sure to ask a hospital staff member to let you know if he seemed out of sorts after your visit. If this was the case, carefully consider the pros and cons of ongoing visits in terms of your dog's well being and your own peace of mind.

" He took my heart and ran with it, and I hope he's running still, fast and strong, a piece of my heart bound up with his forever."

—PATRICIA MCCONNELL, *FOR THE LOVE OF A DOG*

Being With Your Dog at the Very End of His Life

If you are reading this book I suspect that you have already loved and lost a special dog, and you've learned that the end of life isn't typically a simple and easy process. Some dogs pass away peacefully in their sleep, but such an uncomplicated passage is certainly the exception. For most dogs, the end of life comes via euthanasia- a purposeful, compassionate act performed with the intent to alleviate suffering. Home hospice care, a means to control pain and provide physical and emotional comfort for terminally ill animals as they decline, is becoming more mainstream. A dog receiving hospice care may die a natural death or, at some point, the family may opt for euthanasia. For more detailed information about end-of-life decision-making, choices associated with the euthanasia process, and hospice care I encourage you to read the very last chapter in *Speaking for Spot*.

If you wish to be by your dog's side when he passes away, know that this is a perfectly reasonable expectation. If the thought of witnessing his very last breath feels emotionally overwhelming, know that it's okay; you are definitely not alone in the way you feel. Consider asking a family member, friend, or a hospital staff member to fill in on your behalf; someone who will provide lots of petting, loving, and doggie treats.

Just as with the loss of any loved one, grief following the death of a beloved pet is often profound. Some people get "stuck" in the grieving process because of the guilt they experience, having missed out on being with their dog when he passed away. Don't let that "stuck person" be you. Determine in advance if you will want to be with your best buddy at the very end of his life. Controlling what you can during this important time period can make the grief process easier, helping you ultimately navigate to an emotional state in which memories of your dear dog elicit smiles rather than tears.

When Your Dog is in the Hospital

If your dog is hospitalized for a serious illness, there is always the possibility, however slight, that he may pass away when you are not there. This rarely happens, especially if the hospital policy is to call you, any time, day or night, the moment your dog's condition significantly declines. Contacting you as soon as change is observed is likely to create enough time for you to get to your dog's side during his final moments. Of course, this is only possible if your dog is receiving round-the-clock care (see chapter two).

Death can be unpredictable and every once in awhile, a patient passes away without clear warning. When this happens and there is no opportunity for that final goodbye, it is heartbreaking for everyone involved, including those who were caring for your dog.

Does this mean you shouldn't hospitalize your seriously ill dog? Not at all. As mentioned above, unanticipated loss of a patient is unusual. However, if your dog's status should suddenly take a turn for the worse, here are some suggestions to ensure that you get to the hospital in time:

☛ Have a heart-to-heart talk with your veterinarian about the seriousness of your dog's condition. Does she think it's likely that your dog could pass away while in the hospital? If so, what is her best guess as to when this might occur?

☛ Let the hospital staff know that you wish to be contacted any time, night or day should your dog's condition takes a turn for the worse. Explain that being with him during his final moments is most important to you.

☛ Provide all contact information including the number for the phone that will be under your pillow and set to the loudest ringtone while you are sleeping. You don't want to miss that important phone call.

☛ Visit with your dog as much as the hospital policy allows (see chapter eleven).

☛ Have a frank discussion with your veterinarian about whether or not you would want your dog resuscitated (brought back to life), should he suddenly stop breathing or his heart stop beating. In many cases resuscitation is unsuccessful. Even when successful (breathing and heartbeat restored), many dogs remain unconscious. Those who do regain consciousness rarely survive long term. People who opt for resuscitation do so with ongoing hope for recovery or the desire to allow time for them to get to the hospital and be with their dog when he passes away. Others authorize "do not resuscitate" (DNR) status. Based on your dog's medical status and underlying disease, your vet can help you decide whether or not resuscitation makes sense. And based on how strongly you feel the need to be with your best friend when he takes his final breath, your heart will help you decide whether or not resuscitation makes sense.

Euthanasia

Among the clients I serve, approximately 80 to 90 percent choose to be present during the euthanasia process. I always welcome this for two reasons. First, I sometimes hear regret and guilt voiced by people who chose not to be with their dog during the final moments of his life, whereas clients who remained with their dog are invariably glad they did. Second, unless my patient is unconscious and completely unaware, I believe in my heart of hearts that dogs derive profound security and comfort from the presence of their beloved humans. There are no words that adequately describe the mutual devotion conveyed during those final moments.

Of all the experiences we humans endure, being with a beloved pet during the euthanasia process is certainly one of the most difficult, yet most treasured. If you *do* wish to be with your dog when he is euthanized, please do not take "No" for an answer! I view a veterinarian's refusal to honor this request as unacceptable, and wholeheartedly recommend you find a more progressive care provider. Remember, you only have one chance to get it right.

" Don't accept your dog's admiration as conclusive evidence that you are wonderful."

—ANN LANDERS

What Your Veterinarian Expects From You

The preceding chapters have all addressed what is reasonable for you to expect from your veterinarian. In the spirit of saving the best for the last, this final chapter is devoted to describing what is reasonable for your vet to expect from you! Remember, collaboration is the key ingredient of a successful veterinarian-client relationship!

Below, I've described several expectations. By complying with them, you will make the job of caring for your dog easier and more enjoyable for your veterinarian as well as her staff members. They will sing your praises and roll out the red carpet (or at least make a fresh pot of coffee) every time you arrive for an appointment. In addition to the hospital staff, your efforts to fulfill these expectations will directly benefit your dog's health- and nothing is more important than that!

Reasonable Expectations

☛ Arrive on time for your appointment. An "on time arrival" means that you and your dog are present and accounted for in the waiting room, not in the parking lot finishing up a cell phone conversation or outside walking your best buddy with hopes he will empty his bladder. When you arrive late, not only will you and your dog be shortchanged on time spent with the vet, there's a chance the staff will remain behind schedule for the rest of the day. If you are tempted to arrive late because your vet is consistently tardy, call ahead and chat with a front office staff member who will know if it's reasonable for you to arrive after your scheduled appointment time.

☛ If you and your dog are new to the practice, plan on arriving 10 to 15 minutes early to fill out necessary paperwork. Be sure to bring all prior medical records including doctor's notes, x-rays, EKG (electrocardiogram) tracings, ultrasound reports and images, and laboratory test results. Old invoices are not a substitute for the medical record.

- If you suspect your dog has a contagious disease such as kennel cough or an infectious form of diarrhea, please forewarn the staff. For the sake of other patients in the waiting room, you may be asked to keep your little snookums in the car until it is time for the doc to see him.

- Unless instructed otherwise, do your best to bring your dog in with an empty stomach and a full bladder. This means skipping breakfast, keeping your pup inside for a couple of hours ahead of your appointment time, and foregoing the popular doggie "p-mail" spots outside the clinic. Your vet may want a urine sample for testing and if procedures are recommended, better that breakfast was skipped. Not to worry if your pooch urinates while in the hospital. Guaranteed, he will be neither the first nor the last dog to do so!

- By all means, let the staff know if your dog is aggressive. All animals are capable of unpredictable behavior. A savvy veterinary staff member can usually peg an aggressive dog (or a dog who is so fearful he might bite) within seconds of meeting him. Every once in a while a dog surprises us and bites either a staff member or client without warning. Everyone feels terrible when this happens, but it's made far worse when we learn that the client knew that her dog was aggressive in the past, but failed to warn us.

☛ Please turn off your cell phone. Not only is the ringing phone a distraction, answering it while in the midst of conversation with your veterinarian is disruptive and conjures up adjectives I'd best not mention.

☛ Come prepared to provide a thorough history. Believe it or not, your observations often provide more clues about the underlying diagnosis than the actual physical examination. In fact, a solid history can sometimes make the difference between having to run one diagnostic test versus five. Do some sleuthing around the home front (house, garage, and yard) to make sure there's nothing unusual your dog may have ingested. Your vet will want to know if you've observed any vomiting, abnormal stools, coughing, sneezing, decrease in stamina, or changes in appetite, thirst, or bladder and bowel habits. If you are not in charge of "poop patrol," talk to the person who is!

- Bring along all of your dog's current medications (including supplements, flea control products, and heartworm preventive) so your veterinarian can confirm that everything is as it should be. At a minimum, provide a written list of what you are giving your dog, including the name, strength, and frequency of administration of any medications. A visual description of the tablet doesn't cut it- many different medications come in the form of small, round, blue pills. Yes, the information about your dog's medications may already be in his medical record, but you'd be surprised how often significant, sometimes life threatening discrepancies are discovered simply because someone made an error in the process of prescribing or filling a medication.

- Know the name of the food(s) your dog is eating. One step better, bring along any pet food labels. Not uncommonly, clients can describe the appearance of the dog food bag or wrapper "to a T," but for the life of them, cannot remember the brand name of the product. If your dog is eating a homemade diet, bring along a copy of the recipe.

- Do your best to provide direct answers (without significant embellishment) to the questions asked by your vet. For example, if she asks if you have been filling the water bowl any more or less than usual, try to provide a "yes or no" response. Answers such as, "I give her only bottled water." or "She absolutely adores water. She plays in it every chance she gets!" are interesting, but they fail to provide the information your veterinarian is after.

☛ If your dog is sick, do your best to have all the decision-makers present at the time of the office visit. If this is difficult to arrange, the person present should ideally take notes and even consider audio recording the conversation. When only one decision-maker is present, invariably details become lost or confused in translation. Sometimes the missing decision-maker can be called during the office visit and placed on speakerphone to facilitate a three-way conversation. Having everyone present saves your veterinarian from having to spend time providing the same lengthy explanation and answering the same questions multiple times.

☛ While I know it can be awkward, I strongly encourage you to discuss payment options with a staff member *before* services are provided. What receptionist hasn't heard, "What, you don't take American Express®?" Though most facilities accept cash, credit cards, and checks, there is no standard that applies to all veterinary facilities.

➥ Do your very best to comply with the treatment plan that you and your veterinarian have agreed upon for your dog. If this plan becomes unfeasible for any reason, contact your vet to discuss alternatives rather than taking matters into your own hands.

➥ Treat the entire staff with respect. I get really peeved when I learn that a client, who has been sweet as can be with me, has been abrupt, condescending, or rude to one of my staff members. Keep in mind that every individual who works in the hospital plays an important role in keeping your dog healthy. The receptionist decides whether or not to squeeze your dog in for an emergency appointment at 5:30 on a Friday afternoon. The technician is responsible for monitoring your dog's anesthesia during surgery. The staff member who cleans the hospital is in charge of preventing your dog from leaving the hospital with a disease he didn't have when he arrived. Everyone who works at your vet hospital deserves to be treated with gratitude and respect, and without a doubt, the entire staff will know if this has not been the case. By the same token, delivery of a heartfelt compliment or an expression of gratitude (particularly if accompanied by a plate of homemade goodies) will be shared and appreciated by everyone involved in taking care of that wonderful dog of yours.

" Dogs are not our whole life, but they make our lives whole."

—ROGER CARAS

Index

Made in the USA
Lexington, KY
20 December 2011